The Bleeding Ache

Sharin Ali

BookLeaf Publishing

DEDICATION

To young Sharin, you did everything you could. To everyone struggling with mental health, this is for you. This is for us. You are not alone and someone knows how you feel.

Before you delve into my poetry. I would like to acknowledge that there are topics that could be triggering to some. My poetry talks about heavy subjects such as self-harm, suicide ideation, substance use, depression, anxiety and PTSD. If you or someone you know is struggling please reach out for help.

Crisis Services Canada: 1.833.456.4566 or text 45645

ACKNOWLEDGEMENT

First and foremost I want to thank my best friend Manjot 'Mango' Badesha for believing in me and being by my side at the darkest times. I don't know what I would do without you. I would also like to thank my grade 3-4 teacher Sister Kerry for introducing me to the simile and metaphor. You encouraged me to write and be creative. You celebrated when I made my first metaphor after being confused with the concept. I also couldn't forget to thank my mom for letting me run amok with my imagination and providing me with whatever art supplies we could afford. To everyone else who believed in me, read my writing and was extremely patient with me when asking when I would release a book, this is for you. A special shoutout to my fellow writer and friend, Pooja Raj, who helped get the ball rolling on this project. This would not be completed without you. And Riley Fortin, thank you for putting up with my nonsense. You have no idea how much it means to me. Miigwetch! If I missed anyone else, just know I am extremely thankful you are in my life and followed me on this journey.

PREFACE

To my depression:

You do not own me
You do not define me

but you exhaust me.

I spend all my waking hours fighting you. My
body and mind a battleground between
depression and anxiety. I live in constant fear,
hopeless for a cure for this sadness and despair.

Afraid of abandonment and loneliness, I isolate
myself. Panic consumes me and I have nowhere
to go.

I have no present and no future, just a past that
haunts me and makes this depression linger in
my life. Waiting for me to succeed so it can take
it all away from me.

Loneliness I

loneliness is like a week cracking through the pavement

breathing through suffocation the days bring

passing me by like a train i tried to run for but missed

again and again.

loneliness is like a thorn wedged into my chest

sometimes i can find the strength to get comfortable with the bleeding ache

that runs down my body like a fault line

fighting to pull away

or a river that forgets its way through the valley

licking its own wounds and mistakes against the smothered walls too hurt to say sorry.

sometimes loneliness is like passing out

when my blood cells are deprived of oxygen its
ok

because i wont feel for a while

but my heart protest because its love has been
deprived

causing cells to die

and the networks to collapse like i do

at the end of the day

after i carry loneliness up too many hills

i tried to let go of it

but it clung onto me and my body

begging me not to let go

because its all i have.

Lonely

I stop myself from letting other people know I'm
lonely
I will always be lonely
and i should learn to live with it and make it my
friend
it doesn't matter where i am or who i am with
loneliness is always in the background
like a song whispering through a party
as people communicate and share stories
laughing and gasping when appropriate
it taps me on the shoulder when I'm doing well
reminds me of my failure to connect with others
that surround me
i like to think that I'm a lost cause
as loneliness always catches up with me
no matter where i am
it finds me when I'm most vulnerable
anywhere, everywhere and nowhere
i try not to care or let it bother me
but it finds a way through my bones
and makes it s home there
in a place where strength prevails
loneliness hails.

Homesick

I feel homesick although I'm home
the houses grow faster than the mountains
and the gardens bloom dead
as i guide my hands along the cave of my hall
into a solemn submarine
where i shower off sleep and faded possibilities
I never tried.
as the sun puckers into a raisin
there are only so many movements i can make
lying in bed
hallucinations make dreams vivid
as the numbers on the clock jolt
turn into wasted figures and chances
they become tucked into my alveoli
in hopes
of keeping hope alive.

Chances

How do you know it's your only chance?
that maybe the last words that were said hung in
the room like quotation marks
were you last chance
or how the last time you had dinner with
someone
you felt like you were becoming the past
it left you wondering why you tried to
reciprocate yourself
wringing your heart out over and over
trying to give all your love away because you
feel its true
and they leave you slowly as the night paints
itself
into the lonely lit streets you find yourself on
night after night wondering at what time
the change to leave presented itself
before it broke.

Phantom Limb

Its funny how someone can trickle into your
thoughts
and stream through you
leaving you to sink as if they were rocks in a
river
i still find it funny how you treated me like i was
a limb
how could you dispose of me so easy
Was it hard?
Taking me apart
ripping me apart from you
like i was a limb you never needed
Do I haunt you?
Because i feel your loss when i come to the city
your heart beat no longer murmurs and gushes
its phrases out into the crowds
it ceased to exist as you left
and barred me out someplace else
its funny because im over yourself but the
brashness of the past
scours my ability to forgot
how you tore me apart
and left me hanging
like a limb.

Pedestal

7

I put you on a pedestal so high
that when you fell
i wasn't the only thing that broke your fall
but all my love for you too.

Burden of Sadness (Ghost of a Girl)

I feel like such a burden
because sadness is the heaviest emotion to carry
around
it's like a dead body
you forgot to dispose of
and it decays inside of you
leaving the bones of a person
you used to be
before sadness danced into your life
one night when you were in bed
thinking of all the thing you could have been by
now
and you still lay there
heavy and hopeless
no matter how many times
you shift around in bed
you cant shake it off your sheets
or out of your hair
it just lays there beside you
like the ghost of a girl
who had it all once.

Flooded Embankments

I watched your eyes turn into flooded
embankments
overflowing all the feelings you couldn't hold in
anymore
you thought you could hold it all inside
that when you shut your eyes
they became sandbags
holding back the dam of all the unspoken truths
you wanted to expose but couldn't
who would hold you when you flood the space
between the two of you
drowning yourself
and the other person with you.
they'll leave anyways
so you hold all the feelings inside
until it rains so hard inside
that your head can't take it anymore
and you burst through all the dams you built
to hold in the truth.

Demands of Drowning

You'd think drowning would get easier
that our lungs already partially filled by water
could take on more
that the more you lose touch with yourself
is like drowning away
all the plans you had for yourself
washed away by the crashing waves
from the storms stirred up
by life and all its demands
leaves you sinking
closer to the person
you used to be.

Sleepless

When i ward of sleep
the night becomes a long hallway i try to avoid
loneliness turns time into water
where it slips away from me.

Inner Child

12

I feel you drifting to me when i try to sleep
i feel your pain falling down my face
emptying onto my chest
the wound peels back
and i carry pain for two stillborn people
just wanting to grow.

Beast

You can't save her
from the beasts in the night
she lies in bed and screams
because that's all she can do
pleading for help that never comes
all the excuses she hears from others
are that they are too busy saving themselves to
care
so she screams as the pain writhes in her
sometimes she wishes she can bleed it out
drown out the sounds in her head
but she can't get herself to draw the first line
because she feels too much
inside and outside
when she wants to feel she can't
and when she runs away she's stuck
burning in a hell
that no one understands.

The Bleeding Ache

Sometimes i want to take a knife to the chest
and drive it through my sternum
and down my womb
breaking through bones that have become soft
with every heaving breath leaving my lungs
bruising my ribs
sorrow comes out in wails
from the grave my body becomes
opening up a wound that is visible to me
and no one else
the pain unable to be housed in this vessel
becomes a bleed throughout my body
that cannot be stopped.
I stand in the distance
away from it all
fall to my knees
beneath it all
and let the madness trail behind me
because i know i can't out run it
it comes to me
before i have a head start.

Sometimes I Sleep with Smirnoff

Vodka makes me feel like
what love is
late at night
i take straight passive shots
and feel it burn through my body
it warms my face
like two hands cupping my cheeks
to the side of someone's face
to theirs
my mind in a loving haze of after sex
and virginal thoughts
the damning truth baptizing my soul
that no one wants me
as I lie on the floor.
If i was wanted
i would be laying in bed
beside someone other than Smirnoff.

Medication

This medication makes my subconscious tell me
stories while i sleep
every night
i lay abandoned and bruised
like the sun before it rises
left to lick its wounds
in the promise it needs to bring the morning
i lay in bed mourning all the relationships lost
and i don't know whose fault it is anymore
but i regret not saying 'i love you'
even though
I know it means nothing.

I love you
rolls off my tongue
and down the sides of this house
and into the gutter
where I lay waiting...

for when i will wake up
and shake this sadness from my head
instead
i think about sticking my head through the wall
in hopes of seeing the other side

and re-balance the chemicals in my brain again.

Maybe i can be normal again
and try to have a life like you
and everyone else.

Presence/ Present

I struggle to stay in the present
when i can't feel my own presence in the room.

For Your Information

I regret to inform you
that its not my fault
 i'm doing the best i can
with nothing
im making something
out of nothing
and your foolish to judge me so quickly
when you can barely look yourself in the eyes
when you belittle me
i'm holding back natural disasters
that spill from my skin
i let them go when i'm alone
i know no one is coming for me
even though my body is a state of emergency
i lay bloated on the bathroom floor
bathing in my own blood
soaking in a rain
unleashed from this pain
too real to feel in this vessel
i transcend
between a place
somewhere away from here.

Body of Water

i lay in bed at 10:24pm
my body in some dark ocean
i cant see around me
and i know I'm alone
I'm too tired to cry out
because i know it's not worth expending the
energy
to try and see if anyone is out there.

Its 4:41 a.m. and i still lay there
lost in some abyss
there is no light in the dark
and i'm too tired to bat my eyelashes
and move my body to the other side.

It's 9 a.m.
i still lay there empty
my bed sheets produce no evidence
that anyone is alive ehre
as i lay there
unsure if i exist.

Invisible Illness

It's been an hour since I got up abruptly
all because my mind couldn't stay quiet long
enough to succumb to sleep
I woke up with my heart slamming me against
the bed
my body stumbling underneath it
writhing on the bathroom floor
my cheeks kissing the concrete tiles
looking for salvation from this fever
sweeping over my body on fire
my sweat tries to douse the flames
I feel my stomach crawling out of my mouth
as I lay on the floor unable to move
my heavy heart beating me down
as my body takes flight
I feel relief rain over me
as i shiver with dizziness
I get up and go back to bed
like I was never sick
some phantom illness that possessed my body
leaving no indication
that I will ever heal.

Nausea

I learned how to spell nausea so well
because its all I know
I try not to spill the contents of my stomach
into a porcelain ocean
as I grapple with trying to ride the wave of the
moment
as sea too choppy for my own liking
I feel it rise
my internal thermometer
meeting a breaking point
only to stay staggered at the top
too stubborn to let it go
I'm left on my knees waiting
for nausea to pass
so I can get on with my day.

This Room

I can't tell you what sets off my body in this
room
I don't know why my body doesnt think
something isn't right here
I can feel the fog coming for me
my ears are ringing
my eyes glazing over
blurring everything in front of me
I'm blazing hot and the heat rises
I can feel my heart pounding a warning to leave
this place
I'm afraid I'm going to swallow my tongue
for real this time
I feel it turn to sandpaper in my mouth
begging for water, holding an ocean of guilt
down
I stumble out of my chair and my movement
feels so animated
reaching for my coat, phone, medication and
peppermint oil
I feel like everyone can tell I'm losing my shit
and it makes leaving even more inevitable
I shuffle through the rows feeling like I'm not
going to make it to the door

When I get there I'm unsure how to turn the
handle
and I can feel the room looking at me fumble
around
I become a wounded animal looking for shelter
from wounds inflicted by someone else
staggering through the hallway looking for fresh
air
a pasture to die
I somehow make it down the staircase
into the atrium
I feel so exposed in this crowded place
I make it outdoors somehow
and I close my eyes and finally breathe
feel the burden of the room leaving me
I don't know if I can go back
to a place I can't relax
unaware of how I'm being destroyed
right in front of you.

www.ingramcontent.com/pod-product-compliance
Lightning Source LLC
Chambersburg PA
CBHW070727160726
48003CB00006BA/2402